BE NOT AFRAID
How To Conquer Your Fears

BE NOT AFRAID
How To Conquer Your Fears

ISBN 1-931727-94-5

Copyright © 2003 by Celebration Enterprises
P.O. Box 1045, Roswell, GA 30077-1045

SYNERGY PUBLISHERS
Gainesville, Florida 32635

BE NOT AFRAID

How To Conquer Your Fears

BOB GASS
with Ruth Gass Halliday

Scriptures Used

All Scripture used in this book are King James Version unless otherwise indicated.

Scripture quotations marked AMP are taken from *The Amplified Bible, Old Testament.* Copyright © 1965, 1987 by the Zondervan Corporation. *The Amplified New Testament*, copyright © 1954, 1958, 1987 by the Lockman Foundation. Used by permission.

Scripture quotations marked CEV are taken from the *Contemporary English Version*, copyright © 1995, 1999 by American Bible Society, New York. Used by permission.

Scripture quotations marked NAS are from the *New American Standard Bible.* Copyright © 1960, 1962, 1963, 1968, 1971, 1972, 1975, 1977 by the Lockman Foundation. Used by permission.

Scripture quotations marked NCV are taken from *The Holy Bible, New Century Version*, copyright © 1987, 1988, 1991 by Word Publishing, Dallas, Texas 75234. Used by permission.

Scripture quotations marked NIV are taken from the *Holy Bible: New International Version.* Copyright © 1973, 1978, 1984 by the International Bible Society. Used by permission of Zondervan Bible Publishers.

Scripture quotations marked NLT are taken from the *Holy Bible, New Living Translation*, copyright © 1996. Used by permission of Tyndale House Publishers, Inc., Wheaton, Illinois 60189. All rights reserved.

Scripture quotations marked NKJV are taken from the *New King James Version.* Copyright ©1979, 1980, 1982, Thomas Nelson Inc., Publishers. Used by permission.

Scripture quotations marked TLB are from *The Living Bible.* Copyright © 1971 by Tyndale House Publishers, Wheaton, IL. Used by permission.

Scripture quotations marked TM are from *The Message: The New Testament, Psalms and Proverbs.* Copyright © 1993, 1994, 1995, 1996 by Eugene H. Peterson. Used by permission of NavPress Publishing Group.

TABLE OF CONTENTS

1 Your Alarm Clock 5

2 Fear Facts 13

3 Your Internal Chatterbox 25

4 Procrastination and Indecision 35

5 Fear of Lack 45

6 Fear of Sickness 57

7 Fear of Death 67

8 Expand Your Horizons 77

9 Do It Now! 87

10 Forty Fear-Fighters 91

Acknowledgements 98

When you know with absolute certainty that you're at peace with God, you'll automatically be at peace with yourself and the world around you.

"How can I be at peace with God?" you ask.

Paul answers:
"Therefore being justified by faith, we have peace with God through our Lord Jesus Christ."

ROMANS 5:1

Bottom line: only when you know that you're at peace **with** God, will you be able to enjoy the peace **of** God.

"What kind of peace is that?" you ask.

Again Paul answers:
"God's peace, which is far more wonderful than the human mind can understand...
will keep your thoughts and your hearts quiet and at rest as you trust in Christ Jesus."

PHILIPPIANS 4:7 TLB

*Analyze the situation fearlessly,
figure out the worst that can happen.
Once you've accepted that,
you experience a release of faith
and energy and you can begin
doing something about it,
even if all you can do is…
leave it in the capable and
loving hands of God.*

1
YOUR ALARM CLOCK

Fear is the body's alarm clock. It's designed to forewarn and protect us. One of the reasons we've survived so long is because of our automatic response to it. Your "Fight or Flight" instinct prepares you to confront whatever you fear, or run from it.

But fear can also work against you by triggering worry, distress, terror, shyness, withdrawal, apprehension, timidity, and even dread. It's the underlying cause of anxiety attacks and panic disorders.

Anxiety, which is simply *fear that lacks a specific cause*, is like a stream trickling through your mind. Eventually it creates a channel through which *all* your other thoughts begin to flow. Once that happens, fear signs a long-term lease, unpacks its bags and moves in!

When you live in a constant state of anxiety, rushes of adrenaline over-stimulate your heart, weaken your immune system and leave you vulnerable to illnesses like strokes, heart attacks, chronic fatigue, and even some kinds of cancer.

During the Gulf War in 1991, when Iraq launched Scud missile attacks against Israel, many Israelis died, but not from the Scuds! When the war ended and scientists analyzed the mortality statistics, they discovered something remarkable. Although the death rate jumped dramatically on the first day of the attacks, the majority of people hadn't died from the physical effects of the missiles; they'd died from *heart failure!*

Jesus described the world we live in like this: "It will seem like all hell has broken loose… everyone…in a panic, the wind knocked out of them by the threat of doom, the powers-that-be quaking" (Lk 21:25-26 TM).

In 1990, seven in ten people reported feeling hopeful about the future. But a follow-up survey in 2001 showed that *only one in five* felt the same way. Among the issues that generated fear for them were:

Getting sick and not being able to pay their medical bills: 36%

That their retirement programs will go bust: 35%

Having to care for elderly parents: 31%
Not having any inheritance to pass on to
their children: 22%

That the Stock Market will crash again: 20%

Then when you add terrorist attacks, war,
unemployment, drugs, homelessness and
threatening viruses, you realize we're living in the
world's most fearful generation. You actually get
a better understanding of fear by examining it
within three contexts:

(1) *Things that happen naturally:* like aging,
disability, retirement, loneliness, financial uncertainty, accidents, illness, losing a loved one, and
death.

(2) *Things that require action:* like making
decisions, starting and ending relationships,
losing weight, driving, changing careers, making
a mistake. If any of these sound familiar to you,
it's because fear is so insidious. If for example,
you're fearful about encountering new situations, you'll also be afraid to meet new people,
find yourself in unfamiliar settings, or apply for
jobs outside your field because fear permeates
every area of your life!

(3) *Fears reflecting your inner state of mind:*

like rejection, helplessness, disapproval, failure, stress, and vulnerability. *These fears reveal how you feel about your ability to handle life.* For example, fear of rejection can affect your marriage, your friendships and work associations. In order to avoid being hurt you start shutting others out, your world grows smaller and your opportunities for personal growth become more limited.

These fears underlie *all* the rest, and can be reduced to one question, "What if I can't handle it?" They convince you that you can't cope with growing older, being alone, making decisions, failure (especially financial), sickness, rejection, or death.

Your mind is the battlefield where victory is won or lost. So ask yourself this, "Would I be afraid still if I knew for certain I could handle *anything* that came up?"

Think about that for a second; the answer is *no!* Fear can't immobilize you and steal your joy when you know you can handle whatever happens, right? Sound too simple? Well it's not! Because this is where *God* weighs in. The Bible says that with Him on your team, you can "make it through anything" (Ph 4:13 TM).

Late one night, New York photographer Paul Keating saw two muggers robbing a college student. Without considering his own safety, he tackled them while the victim ran for help. Moments later two shots rang out and Keating lay dead on the pavement. Later when the City posthumously awarded him a medal of heroism for his courage, the Mayor said: "Nobody was watching that night. Nobody made Paul Keating step forward in the time of crisis. He did it because that's the kind of person he was."

What makes somebody courageous anyway?

Think its power? Possessions? Popularity? Think again! If *power* could do it, Joseph Stalin wouldn't have been afraid to go to sleep at night, or been so paranoid that he needed a soldier to guard his very tea bags! If *possessions* could do it, fear wouldn't have caused billionaire Howard Hughes to live like a hermit and die in isolation. If *popularity* could do it, John Lennon's biographers wouldn't have described him as a fearful man who slept with the lights on and was terrified of germs.

The more you focus on your fear, the more fear you experience! Instead, you need to focus on

God; He can empower you to handle *anything* you'll ever face.

If a venomous snake bit you you'd have to take an antidote, or become sick and die. The same is true of fear; the antidote is – faith in God and the promises He's made to you! Jesus said, "I have given you [present possession] authority …over…the enemy…nothing shall…harm you" (Lk 10:19 AMP). Thirty-one times the Bible says we are "in Christ." That means nothing can get to you without first coming through Him.

That's a truth you can build your life on!

"Half the worry in the world
is caused by trying to make decisions
before we have sufficient knowledge
on which to base them. Fifty-percent
of our worries vanish once we've arrived
at a clear definite decision and put it
in writing. Another forty-percent
usually vanish once we decide
to carry out that decision."

2
FEAR FACTS

Hopefully you'll find these lesser-known fear-facts as helpful as I did:

(1) *As long as you keep growing, fear never completely disappears.*

I know that's not what you wanted to hear; you were probably hoping for some inside secret that would make all your fears vanish. But it doesn't work that way and here's why. Any time you grow, stretch, and risk fulfilling your God-given potential, you'll run headlong into fear. It's normal – it lets you know you're still alive. The people who know no fear are not only a gross exaggeration, they're a biological impossibility.

We *all* face times when we must choose between trust and fear! A woman trapped in an abusive relationship must decide between getting help, getting out, or staying stuck. A teenager experiencing pressure to do wrong can choose to go with the crowd, take a stand, or walk away.

An older person fearful about death can read God's Word, talk to somebody about it, or continue to live in dread.

God says, "The righteous are bold as a lion" (Pr 28:1). Now even if you don't feel quite that brave, remember this: *courage isn't the absence of fear, it's the mastery of it!* David said, "Wait on the Lord…and He shall strengthen thine heart" (Ps 27:14). When your cause is right and you commit it to God, He'll give you the boldness you need to act.

(2) *Run towards the roar!*

To trap a gazelle, young lions will hide in the bushes and position an old lion in the open. Now, the old lion doesn't have the speed, stamina, (or the teeth) to kill the gazelle. All he can do is roar! If the gazelle is wise, he'll run *toward* the roar and discover it can't harm him. But if he's afraid he'll run *from* it, right into the pride of young lions and be devoured.

Which way do *you* tend to run?

William Ward says: "Fear is faith in the negative, trust in the unpleasant, assurance of disaster, belief in defeat. It's the magnet that attracts negative conditions. It actually wastes today's time by cluttering up tomorrow's opportunities with yesterday's troubles."

It's the roar that sends us running in the wrong direction every time!

Sam and Jed were fortune hunters who heard about a $5,000 reward being offered for wolves captured alive. After scouring the mountains, Sam awoke one night to find they were surrounded by wolves with flaming eyes and bared teeth. Refusing to give in to fear he nudged his friend and whispered, "Hey Jed, wake up – we're rich!"

It's all in how you look at it!

You must learn to face the thing you fear, because each time you do, it diminishes; plus the fact, it builds self-esteem and assures you that you can overcome the *next* obstacle that arises. It can be as simple as standing up for what you believe, making a phone call you've been putting off, expressing your opinion without trying to placate or impress, acknowledging some sin or character flaw you've been hiding and asking God to help you change. A healthy self-esteem enables you to give and receive, have a sense of humor, embrace new ideas, maintain your peace and dignity under stress, and stay flexible and inventive.

But it's crucial to remember that *doing*, always comes before that *feeling* of increased confidence!

Eleanor Roosevelt said, "You gain strength each time you look fear in the face and refuse to back down. You are able to say to yourself, 'I lived through this, so I can handle that?' In other words, you must *do* the thing you think you cannot do."

Each time you face your fears head-on, you *grow* a little more. But when you allow them to control you, you *die* a little more until eventually you come to see yourself as somebody who can't handle life. When that happens, you incur an internal debt that you spend the rest of your life paying off.

(3) *Just do it afraid!*

When Elisabeth Elliot's husband was killed along with four other missionaries in Ecuador, her life was completely controlled by fear. Every time she began to step out, it stopped her in her tracks. Then one day a friend said something that set her free. She said, "Elisabeth, just do it afraid." After that, she and the sister of one of the murdered missionaries went back to Ecuador and built a great work among the Indian tribes, including those who killed their loved ones.

In Genesis God told Abram, "Pack up your stuff. Leave everyone you know and everything you're comfortable with, and start heading for an unknown destination that I'll show you later" (See Ge 12:1). Wouldn't you be just a *little* apprehensive if He said that to you? So was Abram! That's why God kept saying to him over and over, "Fear not."

In Hebrews, chapter 11, verse 8, we read: "By faith Abraham, when he was called to go …went out, not knowing wither he went."

When I left Ireland at 17 to go to America (1962), I'd no formal theological training. I'd two sermons in a briefcase, twenty-five cents in my pocket and a call of God on my life. I arrived in Houston "not knowing" how things would work out. It was only afterwards that doors opened, mentors showed up, and finances were provided.

In 1969, I went to Bangor, Maine to accept the pastorate of a church that was thirty years old and had 300 people in attendance. The retiring pastor had decided to stay as part of the congregation, due to the fact that his wife was ill and couldn't be moved. Most of my pastor friends advised me not to accept the assignment. But I knew I was "called" to it! So I went "not knowing" how it would all work out. When I left that city twelve years later, a new church sat on thirty-two choice acres, an educational building housed a school for 300 children, and 1,500 people attended the two Sunday morning services.

In 1993, when I wrote my first devotional and United Christian Broadcasters in Britain published 3,000 copies, I had no idea that ten years later we'd be publishing approximately eight million copies each year. I just felt "called" to do it. Had I stopped to consider the challenge of writing something fresh for every day of every month of every year from that time forth, fear might well have stopped me in my tracks. So I began, "not knowing" where the road would lead.

In 1955 Rosa Parks, the mother of the civil rights movement, was arrested for refusing to give up her seat on a bus to a white man. Boycotts and protests followed until the Supreme Court ruled that racial segregation was unconstitutional. In *Quiet Strength*, Rosa writes: "When I sat down on the bus that day, I'd no idea history was being made. I was only thinking of getting home. But I had my mind made up. After so many years of being a victim of the mistreatment my people suffered, not giving up my seat, and whatever I had to face afterwards, wasn't important. I felt the Lord would give me the strength to endure it. It was time for someone to stand up – or in my case, sit down."

Do you find yourself wishing you could be one of those brave souls who "grab life by the horns?" If so, here's a news flash! Those folks feel the *same* fear you experience each time you tackle something new! The only difference is, they refuse to let it paralyze them! One successful executive put it this way: "I can't remember *not* being afraid, but it never occurred to me to let it stop me. Instead of seeing fear as a red light to stop, I take it as a green light to move ahead."

You need to develop that same attitude!

David says, *"When I am afraid, I will put my confidence in you...I will trust the promises of God. And since I am trusting him, what can mere man do to me?"* (Ps 56:3-4 TLB). When your mouth is dry, your palms sweaty, your knees knocking and you feel like you're about to keel over, pause and pray: "Lord, strengthen me. This is what You've told me to do, and with Your help I'm going to do it. My life isn't going to be ruled by fear." Then get moving!

(4) *The fear of something is always worse than the thing itself.*

Alice was a homemaker who'd been married for 30 years to Richard, a businessman. Because he'd always taken care of things, she'd learned never to take risks. As a result, Alice's biggest fear was that she'd be left alone. Sound familiar? She would often tell friends, "I hope I go before Richard, because I couldn't handle things on my own."

However, when Richard had a stroke Alice was placed in the position of having to care for him, plus make all the decisions for them both. It was nerve-wracking at first. She was terrified! But once she began to take charge, she made an interesting discovery. Security doesn't lie in *having* things, but in *handling* them! She found that facing her fears was *easy* compared to the years she'd spent feeling inadequate, helpless, and dependent.

Facing your fears is always easier than living with helplessness!

In fact, when you let fear stop you from taking action, you end up living with feelings of dread and helplessness that are ten times *worse*, than if you'd just faced your fears and moved beyond them!

In Genesis, "God called to Adam, 'Where are you?' He replied, 'I hid. I was afraid'" (Ge 3:9-10 NLT). And we've *all* been hiding ever since. "Hiding from what?" you ask. Demanding bosses, controlling spouses, touchy co-workers, strong-willed kids. The list is endless. We hide behind forced smiles, agreeable words we don't really believe and social rituals we detest. Or worse – we hide behind things we *do* believe, but are afraid to say because of what people might think. We also fear the pain that comes from conflict, not to mention the emotional energy we'll have to invest afterwards in the clean up.

Each time fear makes you remain silent in order to avoid conflict, you end up avoiding something more important – *intimacy and integrity!* For example: employees who don't speak up because they're afraid to make waves, often end up alienated from their employers and work mates; husbands and wives who are afraid to confront each other (and this should only be done in love) end up emotionally distanced; Christians who don't share their faith because they fear rejection, lose a priceless opportunity to bring hope to those who need it the most.

So ask yourself, "What am I hiding from today?" Then begin to take action and change it!

(5) *You reap great rewards from courage and obedience.*

The most frequently repeated command in the Bible isn't about pride, humility, sexual purity, integrity, or even love. As important as those are, it's "Fear not," which simply means, "Don't run!" It shows up 366 times in your Bible – one for every day of the year, including leap year! Listen: "Fear not; stand still (firm, confident, undismayed) and see the salvation [deliverance] of the Lord which He will work for you today" (Ex 14:13 AMP).

God continually encourages you because He doesn't want the enemy to steal your blessing. He exhorts you to press on because He knows what awaits you on the other side of the trial.

God told Abram, "Fear not… I am your Shield, your abundant compensation, and your reward shall be exceedingly great" (Ge 15:1 AMP). Now if Abram had buckled, the rest of his story would never have been written. He'd have missed out on his exceedingly great reward.

Don't let that happen to you!

Concerning Satan, the source of most of our fears, the Bible says, "There is no truth in him. When he speaks…he is a liar…and the father of lies" (Jn 8:44 AMP). Satan will use every trick in the book to make you fearful and rob you of God's best. Don't let him!

Obey God – even if you have to do it afraid!

*"God is managing affairs and He doesn't
need any advice from me.
With Him in charge, I believe that
everything will work
out for the best in the end.
So what is there to worry about?"*

HENRY FORD

3
YOUR INTERNAL CHATTERBOX

Each one of us has *an internal chatterbox*. It holds the key to all our fears! It's the little voice that says: "I'd love to have a better relationship, but if I make the first move and they get angry or don't respond, I'll feel rejected again." Or, "I'd really love to go back to school and get my degree, but if I sign up and can't do the work I'll look foolish." Or, "I know a physical exam makes sense, but I'm afraid of what they might discover, so I won't bother going to the doctor."

Some of us are so afraid to be alone with our inner voice that we keep the radio or TV on to drown it out. Others become so used to it that they no longer notice it.

But the fact remains – until we learn to replace our negative self-talk with faith-talk, we'll *always* live in fear!

At his self-esteem seminars Dr. Jack Canfield demonstrates how our internal chatterbox influences *all* we do. Asking a volunteer to face the class he tells her to make a fist, while extending one arm out to the side. Instructing her to resist him as hard as possible, Canfield attempts to push her arm back down again. He's never *once* succeeded! Next, he has the volunteer close her eyes and keep repeating the phrase: "I am a weak and unworthy person," until the negativity of the statement really sinks in. Not surprisingly, he can bring her arm down almost effortlessly. It's as if the person's strength has completely gone.

So what's the bottom line?

Simply this – weak words mean a weak arm; strong words mean a strong arm! And the surprising part is, it doesn't matter whether or not you even *believe* the words. Your inner self doesn't know what's true or false. Whatever you say, it accepts. It never judges. It just reacts to whatever it's fed! That's why Solomon wrote: "For as [he] thinketh in his heart, so is he" (Pr 23:7).

Your mind is like "a placenta," it nurtures any seed you sow. So if you don't want what a seed will ultimately produce, you must either abort it before it comes to full term, or refuse to plant it in the first place. Likewise, if you don't want fear to rule your life, stop rehearsing those thoughts that negatively affect your perception, your moods, your attitudes, your words, and your actions!

"What can I do?" you say.

Ask the Holy Spirit to reconstruct your mind; to put *His* thoughts within you and excommunicate any thought that hinders you from becoming what God wants you to be. By changing your thoughts you can change your world. But it's hard work. It takes commitment!

The trouble is, we all want to be overcomers – without actually having to overcome anything!

Every morning when you shower, shave, fix your hair and get dressed, you know you'll have to do it all again tomorrow. So why bother? Because it's refreshing! It makes you feel better! And so does faith-talk. It's empowering! It feels good! Paul says, "Put on God's whole armor… that you may…successfully…stand up against [all] the strategies and the deceits of the devil" (Ep 6:11 AMP). It's no good just carrying the armor around with you, you must *put it on*.

"How do I do that?" you ask.

By spending time in God's Word! Paul writes: "Scripture is...to teach us what is true and to make us realize what is wrong in our lives. It straightens us out" (2 Ti 3:16 NLT). Allow God's thoughts to correct your thoughts, direct your steps, and straighten you out.

If you struggle with some of the language in the King James Version, try one that's easy-to-understand. And when something really hits you, highlight it, jot down your thoughts, then keep going back and re-reading it until it gets down into your spirit and starts to replace your old stinkin' thinkin'.

Since we're not slow learners but quick forgetters, get some index cards and fill them with fear-fighting Scriptures that really help you, (or use the last chapter in this book). Place them on your nightstand, bathroom mirror, refrigerator, dashboard, or wherever you'll see them constantly.

You can't just *wish* fear away; you've got to *deal* with it!

Instead of complaining about the time you spend driving to and from work, turn your car into a learning center by listening to faith-building, life-giving words. Get a portable player for those times when you're not in the car and carry it with you while you're exercising, gardening, or working around the house.

The Bible says, "God...calls those things which do not exist as though they did" (Ro 4:17 NKJV). And *you* can do that too, through scriptural affirmations! "What are they?" you ask. God's opinion – which is the only one that counts! One reason scriptural affirmations are so effective, is because they're statements about what's happening in your life *right now*, not some future date. Paul says, "I can make it through anything, in the One who makes me who I am" (Ph 4:13 TM). That's an affirmation! David said, "Those who know your name will trust in you, for you, Lord, have never forsaken those who seek you" (Ps 9:10 NIV). That's an affirmation!

Job writes: "Decree a thing, and it will be established for you" (Job 22:28 NASB). As long as your affirmation is scripturally-based, it can be as simple as declaring, "Today I replace my negative self-talk with faith-talk. Today God is filling my life with peace, joy, love, health, abundance and happiness." Practice your affirmations *at least ten minutes a day*, and any other time the enemy starts introducing fear-based thinking.

William Jordan says, "The worst liars are our own fears. They dampen our powder and weaken our aim." But when you speak God's Word into your situation, it brings life and change. You'll be amazed how you can alter your outlook by using – Bible-breathed responses!

Paul writes: "The word that saves is…as near as the tongue in your mouth…[it] welcomes God to go to work and set things right for us" (Ro 10:8 TM). You initiate things by the words you speak. What's created *spiritually*, eventually manifests itself *physically*.

Jesus said, "You…have complete…access to…keys to open any and every door…A yes on earth is a yes in heaven. A no on earth is a no in heaven" (Mt 16:19 TM). The one who has the keys has the authority, and God has given *you* the keys to bring to pass His will on earth. That's powerful!

As a child of God the only confession you should have about fear is that: (a) it's not from God; (b) you won't let it control you; (c) you'll confront it every time with God's Word.

In the Bible the word "confession" comes from the word *homologia*, which means "to say the same thing." Scriptural confession is literally saying the same thing God says, no matter how bad things look. If it's *not* what God's saying, it does no good. But when it is – watch out! It becomes your most powerful weapon in fighting fear!

Solomon writes: "You are trapped by your own words" (Pr 6:2 NCV). Some words are destructive, others are liberating. For example: (a) "What'll I do?" versus "In God's strength I can handle it!" (b) "It's awful!" versus, "It's a learning experience." (c) "I see no way out!" versus "It's not too big for God!"

When the Bible says, "How forcible are right words" (Job 6:25), the word forcible comes from the word *marats*, which means, "to press." In the same way a king's signet ring presses his seal on to a document giving it power, so God's Word on your lips "seals the matter," and releases the power to bring it to pass.

Listen again: "The words of the wise are as...nails fastened by the masters of assemblies"

(Ecc 12:11). Right words hold God's promises in place, so that He can put things together for you.

So, in order to move from fear to faith, you must start eliminating all unscriptural sentiment from your vocabulary. David prayed, "Let the words of my mouth…be acceptable in Your sight, O Lord" (Ps 19:14 AMP).

Make that your prayer too!

*How much does the thing
I'm worrying about really matter to me?
At what point should I put a
"stop-loss" order on it – and forget it?
How much am I willing to pay in terms
of anxiety? Have I already paid more
than it's worth?*

4
PROCRASTINATION AND INDECISION

James writes: "A double-minded man is unstable in all his ways" (Jas 1:8). Indecision is debilitating and habit-forming; it feeds on itself. Not only that, it's contagious; it transmits itself to others.

Your decisions determine your destiny!

Every accomplishment great or small starts with a decision! The Bible says, "If the trumpet does not sound a clear call, who will get ready for battle?" (1 Co 14:8 NIV), because the fear of deciding, can make you hesitate and miss your opportunity.

But what happens if all your life you've been *cautioned* never to make a wrong decision about friendships, finances, education, career, marriage, children. Now you're like the donkey standing between two bales of hay; unable to decide which one to eat, you starve to death! The Bible says, "If you don't take your stand in faith, you won't have a leg to stand on" (Is 7:9 TM).

Often it's our need for *perfection* and *control* that keeps us stuck!

Winston Churchill said: "The maxim, 'Nothing avails but perfection,' may also be spelled paralysis." Henry Ward Beecher wrote, "I don't like cold, precise, perfect people who, in order not to do wrong, never do anything." Too much analysis leads to paralysis. Whenever you're immobilized by the prospect of making a wrong decision, it's generally because you've forgotten one very important principle – you learn from your mistakes!

Here are a few pointers to keep in mind when you're afraid to make a decision:

(1) *You can't please everybody, so stop trying!*

When King Tut's tomb was discovered in Egypt, the walls contained warnings as to the fate of those who disturbed this ancient burial site. Over the next ten years, twenty-plus workers died suddenly or mysteriously. Call it a curse or a coincidence, but what we're talking about here is – the powerful effect of other people's influence! It has the ability to make you believe, and act accordingly. You see it in how you instinctively react to a look or a smile or a frown. The underlying message of disapproval, control, manipulation and condemnation, can send you into a tailspin!

It's good to strive for harmony, but God's Word says, "Do not change yourselves to be like…people…be changed within by a new way of thinking" (Ro 12:2 NCV). Fear will make you try to *become* what you think is acceptable to others. But when you do, their praise is hollow because deep down you're thinking, "You're just admiring what I wanted you to see. If you knew the *real* me you wouldn't respect me at all." Look out: the Bible says, "The fear of man is a dangerous trap" (Pr 29:25 TLB).

(2) *The greatest mistake you can make, is to be afraid of making a mistake.*

There are lots of ways to fail, but *never* taking a chance is the most successful! Roger Von Oech says, "There are two benefits of failure. First: you learn what doesn't work. Second: it gives you the opportunity to try a new approach." Most of us think success and failure are direct opposites, but actually they're just two sides of the same coin. Success isn't necessarily permanent, and failure isn't necessarily fatal. Defeats are just installments on the way to victory! That's why John Maxwell writes: "Fail early, fail often, and always fail forward."

(3) *Do your homework.*

When you're making any major decision it's wise to consider all your options, then talk them over with the *right* people. Mark Twain said, "Keep away from people who try to belittle your ambitions. Small people always do that, but the really great ones make you feel that you, too, can become great." Find people who are knowledgeable, especially those who've solved the same problem, succeeded in the same area, and are willing to help you.

Above all, never hesitate to talk about your plans because you're afraid they won't work out, or that you'll end up looking stupid. Swallow your pride! Failing doesn't make you a failure, quitting does, not learning does, failing to see beyond it does!

(4) *Learn to trust the voice within.*

Isaiah writes: "Thine ears shall hear a word behind thee, saying, This is the way, walk ye in it" (Isa 30:21). Even when you've prayed about your decision, done your homework, consulted the experts, established your priorities and made what appears to be the best choice, if something in your spiritual gut says not to proceed – pay attention. Solomon writes: "Commit to the Lord whatever you do, and your plans will succeed" (Pr 16:3 TLB). And David adds: "We should make plans, counting on God to direct us" (Pr 16:9 TLB). Henry Ward Beecher put it like this, "The strength of a man consists in finding out which way God is going, then going that way himself." During The Civil War, Abraham Lincoln was asked if he was sure God was on his side. He replied: "I haven't really thought about it, I'm more concerned with whether or not I'm on God's side!"

And one more thought: "He that believeth shall not make haste" (Is 28:16). God has your whole life in mind, not just tomorrow. So adopt His pace and don't rush things. David said, "The steps [and stops!] of a good man are ordered by the Lord" (Ps 37:23).

(5) *Lighten up!*

We live in a culture where everything's a big deal! Learn to chill out and stop taking yourself so seriously! Welcome the unknown with cheer, not fear! Flexible people don't get bent out of shape. Whatever the results of their decision, they know that by God's grace they can handle it, and if need be, correct it! *So what* if you make a bad investment – you'll survive, maybe even learn from it and go on to thrive. *So what* if you choose the wrong job, or the wrong house, or the wrong car, or the wrong date? You can usually get another one, right? Paul says, "All that happens to us is working for our good if we love God and are fitting into his plans" (Ro 8:28 TLB). Choose to see yourself as a student in the University of Life and turn all your experiences into higher learning!

(6) *Let it go.*

Anytime you make an important decision, faith and fear will both sail into your harbor. Allow only faith to drop anchor! Paul said, "Forgetting what is behind...I press on" (Ph 3:13-14 NIV). Once the die's cast, let it go and keep looking ahead. It's normal to have expectations of how you'd like things to turn out. But you can't control the future or change the past. Unfulfilled expectations only create misery. Plus, when you're overly focused on the way things *should* be, you miss out on the way they *are* – which most of the time is better than you hoped for.

(7) *Accept responsibility.*

When things don't work out we've a tendency to become fearful and look for somebody to blame. One woman said, "I hated my stockbroker when the stock he recommended went down. It took humility to admit that *I'd* made the decision to buy; nobody twisted my arm. I lamented until I created an "opportunity" from my ill-fated decision. What did I learn? A lot! (a) I needed to research the market for myself instead of always relying on others. (b) I was insecure about money and needed to work on that. (c) Losing money in the future won't be such a big deal, because stocks go back up, like mine did later. Viewed in that light, it wasn't a bad decision after all." When you can find the *opportunity* in any decision, it's easier to take the responsibility for making it. Plus, you're a lot less angry at the world and yourself!

(8) *Fearless living is a lifestyle won only through practice.*

Fearless people have learned to do what does *not* come easily. They repeatedly confront discomfort, distractions, fear, and act in spite of them. R. H. Macy, founder of Macy's Department Stores, failed at five different professions – whaler, retailer, gold-miner, stockbroker, real estate broker – before he finally succeeded. What sustained him through failure after failure? Two things: purpose and persistence! That's what separates those who achieve, from those who merely dream!

(9) *Never protect what you need to correct.*

Never become so invested in the direction you've chosen, that you let pride and fear keep you on the wrong road. When writer Stewart Emery was in the cockpit of a small plane traveling to Hawaii, he noticed a console that was part of the "inertial guidance system." Its purpose was to get the plane to within 1,000 yards of the runway inside five minutes of the estimated arrival time. So anytime it veered off course the system corrected it and they arrived on time, *in spite of having been off course 90% of the time!* Emery says, "The path from here to where we want to be starts with an error which we correct, which becomes the next error which we correct, which becomes the next error which we correct, etc. The only time we are truly on course, is that moment in the zigzag when we actually cross the true path."

In life, the trick is to stop worrying about making a wrong decision and instead learn when to correct. Change courses – even if it means taking heat from those who question your decision. "What do you mean you're canceling the wedding? What about all the money we've spent!" Or, "Why switch majors in your senior year? Think of all the time you've wasted!"

Because the quality of your life is at stake!

"Would you take a million dollars
for what you have?
No?
Then you're rich!"

5
FEAR OF LACK

"My God shall supply all your needs."
PHILIPPIANS 4:19

God will use different methods at different times to meet different needs in your life.

He provided for the children of Israel in *four* different ways: through Pharaoh (the hand of man); through the manna (the hand of God); through the work of their own hands; and through their enemies. Let's look at each and see what we can learn.

(a) Through Pharaoh *(the hand of man).*

When famine hit, God led His people down to Egypt and made Pharaoh take care of them for four hundred years. Get this: when you ask God to meet your needs, don't dictate to Him *who* He'll use to do it! Notice the words of Jesus: "Shall men give into your bosom" (Lk 6:38). *When God wants to bless you, He'll send a person!* But if you're too proud to accept their help, you won't get it. Or if you limit Him to working strictly through people you know and like, you'll miss the boat again.

God used Pharaoh because he's not the type of person you're apt to fall in love with. God doesn't want you getting hooked on anybody but Him! He can bless you through your boss, the taxman, the car dealer, the mortgage lender, or even those who mean you no good! It was betrayal by his brothers that caused Joseph to become Prime Minister of Egypt. People will enter your life and people will leave it. Praise God when they come and praise Him when they go, and remind yourself: "If He blessed me before, He can do it again" – and keep truckin'.

Egypt only became a problem, when God's people stayed there too long! Don't lean on the arm of the flesh too long, or the instrument of your blessing can become an idol. And that's a problem, for God said: "Thou shalt have no other gods before me" (Ex 20:3). Learn to stand on God's Word – and hold everything else lightly! Why? Because God will wean you from dependence on any hand but His. If necessary, He'll allow the Pharaoh who fed you last year to abuse you this year. Then He'll bring you into the wilderness where little or nothing grows, and teach you to trust in Him alone.

(b) Through the manna *(the hand of God)*.

God put the Red Sea between Israel and their old source! Then He introduced them to their new source – manna! Listen: "Thin flakes like frost…appeared on the desert floor. When the Israelites saw it, they said to each other, 'What is it?' For they did not know what is was. Moses said to them, 'It is the bread the Lord has given you" (Ex 16:14-15 NIV). Notice three things:

(1) *At first, you may not recognize your provision.* The word manna means "What is it?" They'd never seen anything like it. It required faith to receive it. Don't be afraid of something just because it doesn't come packaged the way you think it should. Instead say, "Lord, if it's from you I'm going to receive it, thank you for it, enjoy it and start living off it."

(2) *It had to be gathered first thing each morning.* Why? Because by noon the sun had melted it. Before you do anything else go get your manna! Feed yourself on God's Word before the enemy

gets a chance to hit you. Once you've done that you can handle whatever the day brings.

(3) *You receive according to your need, not your neighbor's.* God won't bless you so that you can keep up with the folks in the next tent. If they've got more children to feed, they get more manna! Stop measuring your blessing by what some-body else has. Two things determine the level of your blessing: the amount needed to fulfill your God-given assignment, and the degree to which God can trust you with it. So quit comparing and complaining about what God gave your neighbor, and start being grateful for the "manna" He's placed within your reach.

(c) Through the work of their own hands.

Next we read: "The manna ceased" (Jos 5:12). Some of us fall apart when the manna ceases! "Lord, what's wrong? Nobody's taking care of me anymore!" Nothing's wrong. It's just time to grow up and start believing God to bless you so that you can *become* a blessing to others, instead of constantly asking Him to bless others so they can take care of you! It's time to discover your gifts and start making a difference.

You don't need God or anybody else to do for

you what you can do for yourself!

Listen: "That very day, they ate…the produce of the land: unleavened bread and roasted grain" (Jos 5:11 NIV). How do you get bread and grain? Produce them! God was saying: "I can provide through man or send it from heaven, but now I'm planning to bless the work of your own hands."

You don't require a lot of talent in the wilderness, just faith for your next meal. But here God is saying to His people: "When you enter this land, I want you to live in such a way that the rest of the world will sit up, take notice and start asking, 'What have they got that we don't?'" Instead of us going to the world for advice, they should be coming to us for it! Jesus said, "You are the light of the world" (See Mt 5:14 NIV). That means you should be the brightest student, employee, parent or leader around.

God told His people, "All the nations will call you blessed" (Mal 3:12 NIV). Who's He referring to? Those who unlock their talents, put them to work, and honor God in all they do!

(d) Through their enemies.

There's a fourth way in which God provides

– through your adversaries (and adversities!). Joshua and Caleb stood before the Israelites and said, "Neither fear ye the people of the land; for they are bread for us." Did you get that? There's food in the fight! There are blessings in the battle! You can actually reach a place of maturity where you begin to *feed* off what the enemy throws at you; where your problems become learning experiences that take you to a higher level.

But Israel didn't want to fight. Actually, they wanted to stone those who forced them out of their comfort zone. As a result God said, "Not one of them will ever see the land I promised" (Nu 14:23 NIV). God's greatest pain is to be doubted! With a track record like His, could you blame Him? But are we so different? Before you answer, understand clearly that there are three things you'll *always* have to deal with.

(1) Wanting to stay where you are, because where God wants you to go means confronting family-of-origin fears and conquering old habits the enemy has placed between you and your destiny.

(2) Instead of being confident because of what He's *already* done for you, you walk around

talking like your God is running on one or two cylinders, or is out of contact.

(3) Even though you know the enemy is squatting on your property and defying you to do anything about it, you've no stomach for the fight.

In a moment we'll talk about the enemies *inside the land.* But right now you need to look *inside yourself*, and start dealing with those that have the ability to keep you from enjoying God's best.

Listen: "Because my servant Caleb has a different spirit and follows me wholeheartedly, I will bring him into the land" (Nu 14:24 NIV). Caleb had "a different spirit," one that dared to defy the enemy and say: "We will swallow you up; you're just bread for us" (See Nu 14:9 NIV). Instead of running away, start seeing the growth opportunities in every problem and begin saying, "Bring it on: when the dust settles I'm coming out of this stronger and wiser!"

Have you ever seen jet fighters being refueled in mid-flight? Our God does that too! Just when you're thinking, "I don't know how much longer I can take this," the Holy Spirit comes along side, hooks you up, refills you and makes you an even *bigger* threat to the enemy. It's time you understood how much the enemy fears you, and stop backing down, hiding out, or trying to negotiate a truce with him.

Before Joshua's armies conquered Jericho, Rahab told his spies, "We've heard how the Lord turned the Red Sea into a red carpet and drowned the entire Egyptian army before your eyes" (See Jos 2:10). Your reputation precedes you! The enemy knows you're marked for blessing. *That's what the battle is all about!* Just keep fighting. When God's on your side, problems turn into possibilities! Listen: (a) "God…will soon crush Satan under your feet" (Ro 16:20 NIV). (b) "I give…you power…over all the power of the enemy" (Lk 10:19). (c) Greater is he that is in you, than he that is in the world" (1 Jn 4:4). And there's a whole lot more promises where those came from!

Modern Israel is *still* fighting over the place God gave them 4,000 years ago; a place of permanent provision, of covenant blessings, of such influence that they stay on the front page of every newspaper. And what was a *physical* place in the Old Testament is now a *spiritual* place where every redeemed child of God has been called to dwell.

But it's still a fight!

"The devil isn't bothering me," you say. Maybe that's because you're no threat to him! The moment you get serious about experiencing the abundant life Jesus promised, you're in for a fight!

Did you think the devil was going to send you a congratulatory telegram?

No, listen: "As servants of God we commend ourselves in every way: in great endurance; in troubles, hardships and distresses; in beatings, imprisonments and riots; in hard work, sleepless nights and hunger; in purity, understanding, patience and kindness; in the Holy Spirit and in sincere love; in truthful speech and in the power of God; with weapons of righteousness in the right hand and in the left; through glory and dishonor, bad report and good report; genuine, yet regarded as impostors; known, yet regarded as unknown; dying, and yet we live on; beaten, and yet not killed; sorrowful, yet always rejoicing; poor, yet making many rich; having nothing, and yet possessing everything" (2 Co 6:4-10 NIV).

Maybe you ought to go back and re-read those words several times.

Why?

Because they're "basic requirements" for every citizen who wants to live in, and enjoy the benefits of God's kingdom.

*"Those who don't learn
how to fight worry,
die young!"*

Dr. Alexis Carrel

6
FEAR OF SICKNESS

A well-known internist writes, "Ninety percent of all patients who see physicians have one common symptom. Their trouble didn't start with coughing or chest pain or hypertension. No, the first symptom was *fear!* Sometimes it was nothing more than superficial anxiety. Other times the fear was so deep-seated that the patient denied its existence, taking injections, hormones and tranquilizers in an endless search for relief."

The Bible says, "If ye then, being evil, know how to give good gifts unto your children, how much more shall your Father which is in heaven give good things to them that ask him?" (Mt 7:11). As parents you want your children to enjoy good health, right?

Well, your Heavenly Father wants the same for you!

Why does John write: "I pray that...you may prosper and be in good health, just as your soul prospers"? (3 Jn:2 NASV). Because your physical body thrives in relation to how well you're doing spiritually and emotionally.

If God's been showing you areas you need to deal with in order to be healthy, it's because He loves you! For example, if you're full of resentment it will have a negative effect on your health. Or if you eat junk food all day long and never get off the couch, how can you expect your body to function at its best?

Did you know that there are eight to ten teaspoons of sugar in most soft drinks? By drinking one soft drink daily for ten years, you're ingesting 3,650 teaspoons of sugar. Imagine how that affects you body over time! Diabetes has now moved to the number three slot, just behind heart disease and cancer. And our children are being diagnosed with it in record numbers.

So you have a part to play!

In the Book of Matthew, when Jesus healed a paralyzed man He said: "Your sins are forgiven you" (Mt 9:2 NKJV), and the man was healed. James says, "Confess your sins…and pray for each other so God can heal you" (Jas 5:16 NCV). Why? Because unconfessed sin can be the cause of *some* (but not all) sickness and disease. We live in a world full of germs and viruses that are constantly attacking our immune system, so don't go on a "digging expedition" to figure out what sin might be causing your (or somebody else's) problem. Just stay open to God; He's well able to let you know. It's always interesting that people who are quick to blame *your* sickness on "sin," have a completely different attitude whenever *they* are ill. Never presume to know the reason for somebody else's sickness. Leave that up to God. And remember – mercy is *always* more powerful than judgment!

In the 1870s he terrorized stagecoach travelers without ever firing a shot. His weapon was his reputation, his ammunition was intimidation. He was *Black Bart*, a hooded bandit with a deadly weapon.

And he's not so different from another, more familiar thief. Even though you've never seen him, you'd recognize him in a heartbeat. In the hospital you've felt his cold breath on your neck. He's the one who keeps reminding you, "Your mother had breast cancer, so you'd better keep checking for lumps because you'll get it too." At the cemetery he was the one whispering, "You'll be next." This thief doesn't want your valuables; he wants something more precious – your peace of mind.

His name is "Fear of Sickness." Have you met him?

He manipulates you with the mysterious, and taunts you with the unknown. Fear of routine physical exams, cancer, heart disease, diabetes, death; *especially diseases that "run in your family."*

Paul says, "God hasn't given us a spirit of fear" (see 2 Ti 1:7 AMP). So guess who has?

A 2001 Gallup poll of 1,000 people who'd experienced remarkable physical or emotional healing, revealed that *faith* was the most powerful influence in their lives. Dr. Dale Matthew of Georgetown University, author of *The Faith Factor*, confirms that prayer has great health benefits. He says, "If faith were available in pill form, no pharmacy could stock enough of it!"

John Ortberg cites a medical study in which men who'd suffered their first heart attack were evaluated based on their degree of hopefulness or pessimism. They discovered that of the twenty-five most pessimistic, twenty-one had died eight years later, while of the twenty-five most optimistic, only six had died eight years later! Loss of hope increased the odds of death by more than *three hundred percent!* It predicted death more accurately than any medical risk factor, including blood pressure, the amount of damage to the heart, or cholesterol levels!"

Adding his own inimitable brand of humor, Ortberg says, "Better to eat Twinkies in hope, than broccoli in despair!"

Author Peter McWilliams says, "There are as many examples of how negative thinking helps bring about life-threatening illnesses, as there are people who have them. We each have our own personal list of things that 'push us over the edge.' Fearful thinking provides the opportunity, then the illness takes it from there. Once it takes root, how quickly the illness progresses depends on how much fertilizer we give it from that great manure generator – fearful thinking."

From a *medical* perspective, fearful thinking suppresses your immune system, elevates your blood pressure and causes your stress and fatigue levels to rise. From a *mental* standpoint, it creates the very condition you dread.

For example, it's well known that first-year medical students often assume the symptoms of whatever disease they happen to be studying at the time. Job said, "The thing which I greatly fear comes upon me, and that of which I am afraid befalls me" (Job 3:25 AMP). Plus, the more you believe you're going to get sick and die, the less likely you are to attend to any long-term projects like your career goals and relationships – the very things that give you a reason to live. After a while the question becomes, "What have I got to live for anyhow?" and the subconscious desire to die takes root.

Living with fear is like living with a time bomb strapped to you. If you were told it could go off at any time, you might actually learn to live with it. But if you're told it'll tick 2,000 times before finally exploding, you're constantly doing the math and counting the ticks. Some days it might tick twenty times, other days as much as three hundred times. As long as you count the ticks you experience fear and panic – which is exactly what the enemy wants. Peter writes, "Stay alert. The Devil is poised to pounce, and would like nothing better than to catch you napping. Keep your guard up...*keep a firm grip on...faith"* (1 Pe 5:8-9 TM). The degree to which you're ignorant of Satan's fear-inducing schemes, is the degree to which he can gain a foothold in your thinking and rob you of what's rightfully yours, including your health.

God says, "My people are destroyed from lack of knowledge" (Hos 4:6 NIV). Ignorance can kill you! Too many of us think we can walk to a church alter and have elders lay hands on us with such power, that the enemy will *never* be able to say another word to us. We think if we go to the "right" church or sit under the "right" ministry, we'll become so mature we'll never be fearful again. It won't happen! Why?

Because it's not about making the enemy powerless. It's about making you strong and free!

Freedom from fear means: (a) *you* now control the thing that used to control you; (b) the fear that sat on the throne of your heart has been replaced by faith. It still exists, but it's no longer in charge; (c) fear will try and usurp the throne again. But when it does, it's up to you to resist it, stand on God's Word and exert control with your will. In other words, fear will never stop trying, but God can put you in a position to keep it from succeeding.

Oh, by the way, *Black Bart* turned out to be a mild-mannered pharmacist who was terrified of horses! And the reason he never fired a shot?

His gun was never loaded!

Before leaving this subject, let's take a look at what God has to say concerning the fear of sickness.

(1) "Worship the Lord your God, and his blessing will be on your food and water. I will take away sickness from among you, and none will miscarry or be barren in your land. I will give you a full life span" (Ex 23:25 NIV).

(2) "He forgives all my sins and heals all my diseases; he redeems my life from the pit and crowns me with love and compassion. He satisfies my desires with good things, so that my youth is renewed" (Ps 103:3-5 NIV).

(3) "I will restore you to health and heal your wounds, declares the Lord" (Jer 30:17 NIV).

(4) "Because he loves me, says the Lord, I will rescue him; I will protect him, for he acknowledges my name. He will call upon me, and I will answer him; I will be with him in trouble, and I will deliver and honor him. With

long life will I satisfy him and show him my salvation" (Ps 91:14-16 NIV).

(5) "My son, pay attention to what I say; listen closely to my words. Do not let them out of your sight, keep them within your heart; for they are life to those who find them, and health to a man's whole body" (Pr 4:20-22 NIV).

(6) "When evening came, many were brought to him, and he...healed all the sick. This was to fulfill what was spoken through the prophet Isaiah: 'He took up our infirmities and carried our diseases'" (Mt 8:16-17 NIV).

(7) "He called his twelve disciples to him and gave them authority to drive out evil spirits and to heal every disease and sickness" (Mt 10:1 NIV).

(8) "Is anyone of you sick? He should call the elders of the church to pray over him and anoint him with oil in the name of the Lord. And the prayer offered in faith will make the sick person well; the Lord will raise him up" (Jas 5:14-15 NIV).

(9) "Therefore I tell you, whatever you ask for in prayer, believe that you have received it, and it will be yours" (Mk 11:24 NIV).

"He too shared in their humanity,
so that by his death he might destroy
him who holds the power of death —
that is, the devil — and free those who
all their lives were held in slavery
by their fear of death."

HEBREWS 2:14-15 NIV

7
FEAR OF DEATH

After the 9/11 attacks, a friend of mine was stopped in a supermarket and asked by a neighbor, "Do you know anything about heaven?" She was stunned by the question! *Who* is qualified to answer it? Only somebody who's been to heaven!

And that's two people I know of!

The first is Paul the Apostle. After personally visiting heaven, he described it as, "one huge family reunion." Listen: "We can tell you with complete confidence…that when the Master comes again to get us, those of us who are still alive will not get a jump on the dead and leave them behind. In actual fact, they'll be ahead of us. The Master himself will…come down from heaven and the dead in Christ will rise – they'll go first… the rest of us…will be caught up with them…to meet the Master…then there will be one huge family reunion" (1 Th 4:15-18 TM).

"How can I be sure?" you ask.

Because at the cross a showdown took place. Jesus called Satan's hand. Tired of seeing us intimidated by the fear of death, He walked into the tomb, turned it into a lighted underpass to heaven, came out and announced, "Death, who's afraid of you now?" (1 Co 15:55 TM).

The other person is Jesus. He said, "Let not your heart be troubled; you believe in God, believe also in Me. In My Father's house are many mansions; if it were not so, I would have told you. I go to prepare a place for you. And if I go and prepare a place for you, I will come again and receive you to Myself; that where I am, there you may be also" (Jn 14:1-3 NKJV).

Joe Bayly, who experienced the heartache of losing three of his children, wrote, "I may not long for death, but I surely long for heaven." The loss of our loved ones has that effect on us!

Bayly's insights on heaven are the best I've ever read. Let me share some of them with you:

What will heaven be like? It'll be like moving into a part of your Heavenly Father's house prepared especially for you – no fixing up, no parts unfinished, no disappointments on moving day.

What will we do there? We'll "serve him day

and night" (Rev 7:15). Did you think heaven would be an eternal Sunday afternoon nap? No, you'll have work to do. "Keeping all the gold polished?" No, ruling angels. Managing the universe. Being responsible for whole cities.

"Whole cities? Like London or Chicago?" Like them, but different, because there everybody lives for God's glory, every person safe, like Harlem with trees growing in it, a river of pure water running through it, and people laughing. No sorrow, no pain, no night, no death. (See Rev 21:4).

"Will we meet our loved ones? Will we know them?" Of course; would we know less in heaven than we knew on earth? Didn't Peter, James, and John, know Moses and Elijah on The Mount of Transfiguration? Paul writes, "Face to face…then shall I know even as also I am known" (1 Co 13:12).

"Will our children still be children, and our aging parents still be old?" No. Listen: "…what we will be has not yet been made known. But we know that when he appears, we shall be like him, for we shall see him as he is" (1 Jn 3:2 NIV).

"How about the handicapped?" Jesus said they will be, "Like the angels…children of the resur-

rection" (Lk 20:36 NIV). Paul says God will, "...transform our lowly bodies so that they will be like his glorious body" (Ph 3:21 NIV). Imagine, they'll be whole, able to do everything they couldn't do before! Paul writes: "What we suffer now is *nothing* compared to the glory he will give us later...our full rights as his children, including the new bodies he has promised us" (Ro 8:18 & 23 NLT).

"Will there be anything to worry about there?"

No. No terrorism, bombs, crime, drunkenness, violence, or war. The doors don't have locks on them. All the things that made life fearful for you on earth, will be gone forever. Listen: "There will be no more death or mourning or crying or pain, for the old order of things has passed away" (Rev 21:4 NIV).

"I'm ashamed to admit it, but I'm a little scared. How can I adjust to heaven when it's so different?"

This world is like a womb.

"A womb?"

Yes, just as a baby is bound within the womb, so we are bound by the limitations of this world. Maybe the baby would be scared to be born too, to leave the womb.

"Then death is…?"

"Just a passage from earth life, from the womb that has contained us until now, into the beauty of heaven life. We'll go through a dark tunnel, we may experience momentary pain just as we did when we were born – but beyond the tunnel is heaven."

"Will we all be treated alike?"

No, how you live now, determines what will happen to you after you die. Bruce Wilkinson calls this, "The Law Of The Unbreakable Link." Like the law of gravity, it's always working. The choices you make in your life each day don't come to nothing when you die. They matter! And they'll continue to matter throughout eternity.

Your eternal destination is the result of what you *believe*. Your eternal reward is the result of how you *behave*. Do you agree with that? Really? If you do, it will radically affect: (a) how you think about your life; (b) how you think about God; (c) what you choose to do one minute from now. God wants you to know that the positive consequences of your actions today, can change your eternal prospects in astounding and wonderful ways – and He doesn't want you to waste another minute.

You don't have to worry about what awaits you on the other side of your last heartbeat. Others don't decide that. Even God doesn't – you do! When the truth of that dawns on you, you'll say, "I can't believe I've prepared for my children's future or my old age, but not given a thought to my real future!" Or as one man said, "I've always thought about finishing well, but now it turns out that death is just the starting gate."

You can't do anything about your past, *but starting right now* you can change your future – one choice and one act at a time.

When Jesus was invited to the home of a prominent religious leader, He offered this unsolicited advice. "When you give a dinner or a supper, do not ask your friends, your brothers, your relatives, nor your rich neighbors, lest they also invite you back, and you be repaid…When you give a feast, invite the poor, the maimed, the lame, the blind. And you will be blessed, because they cannot repay you; for you shall be repaid at the resurrection" (Lk 14:12-14 NKJV).

Notice the words, "You will be repaid at the

resurrection." God will repay you for some things *after* you're dead. This contradicts what many of us believe – that God rewards us only on earth. No, Jesus said that when you do a worthy deed for someone who cannot repay you: (a) you will be repaid; (b) much of your reward will come in the next life.

If you fail to understand this you'll find yourself saying: "I serve God faithfully, so why am I struggling? Doesn't God notice or care?" Friend, God notices and God cares! But He doesn't promise that work for Him now, will necessarily result in gain from Him now. Many of the rewards God has for us are so great, it'll take *eternity* to enjoy them!

Jesus said, "Whoever gives you a cup of water to drink in My name…will by no means lose his reward" (Mk 9:41 NKJV). No deed for God will be overlooked or go unrewarded. Not even a cup of cold water, or a prayer in the middle of the night.

But how will God evaluate and reward what we did for Him during our lifetime?

By three tests!

(1) *The test of intimacy!* The life God rewards

is not a life of performance apart from relationship with Him. Jesus said unless we *abide* in Him and *obey* His commands, we will not bear fruit for Him (See Jn 15:5). Jesus commended one church for their good works, then turned around and condemned them because they hadn't kept their love for Him alive. Listen: "I know your works, your labor, your patience... Nevertheless I have this against you, that you have left your first love" (Rev 2:2 & 4 NKJV).

(2) *The test of motive!* Listen: "Take heed that you do not do your charitable deeds before men, to be seen by them. Otherwise, you have no reward...in heaven" (Mt 6:1 NKJV). What should our motive be? To serve God and bring Him glory! On the other hand, our most religious actions are worthless, if our motive is to enhance our own ego and reputation.

(3) *The test of love!* Listen: "Love your enemies, do good, and lend, hoping for nothing in return; and your reward will be great" (Lk 6:35 NKJV). When it comes to good works, *why* is always more important to God than *what!* The Bible warns: "Look to yourselves, that we do not lose those things we worked for, but that we

may receive a full reward" (2 Jn 8 NKJV).

You should constantly pray, "Lord, keep my heart right and my motives pure."

Are you careful or fearful?

Careful is thoughtful;
fearful is emotional.

Careful is fueled by information;
fearful is fueled by imagination.

Careful calculates risk;
fearful avoids risk.

Careful wants to achieve success;
fearful wants to avoid failure.

Careful is concerned about progress;
fearful is concerned about protection.

8
EXPAND YOUR HORIZONS

Dr. Bernard Vittone, an expert in the field of anxiety says: "As we age, we lose the ability to distinguish between the negative anxiety associated with stress, and the positive type that's a natural and exciting part of experiencing something new. As a result we become fearful and try to avoid stressful situations completely, including rewarding ones." When that happens, the desire for safety can cause us to live defensively, never reaching out and never enjoying God's goodness.

Trying to avoid risk is like trying to avoid living; we stop growing altogether!

Just because you're near the top of the hill doesn't mean you've passed your peak! God's oldest were among His finest. The older mellower Abraham was wiser than the brash younger one. Caleb claimed his mountain at 85. Anna, an elderly widow, didn't just pray for the Messiah, she was smart enough to *recognize* Him when He came. On Patmos, isolation became inspiration and old John the Revelator wrote the last book of the Bible.

The voice of *fear* says, "Build a fire in the hearth and stay in where it's warm." But the voice of *faith* says, "Build a fire in your heart, then go out and pursue your passion!"

General Douglas MacArthur said, "You only grow old by deserting your ideals. Years wrinkle the skin but giving up interest wrinkles the soul." Asked why he began studying Greek at age 94, Oliver Wendell Holmes replied, "Well, my good sir, it's now or never!"

You can't test your destiny cautiously. You must be willing to exchange the safety of what you *are*, for what you can *become*. Helen Keller said, "Security is a myth. It doesn't exist. Avoiding danger is no safer in the long run than outright exposure. Life is either a daring adventure, or nothing at all." Smart lady, eh? She's also the one who said, "The only thing that's worse than being blind, is having sight but no vision."

Each of us operates within a realm that feels comfortable. Outside of it we begin to feel uneasy. *You may not be aware of it, but you make most of your decisions based on your comfort zone.*

David said, "I called...and the Lord answered me and set me...in a large place" (Ps 118:5 AMP). Consciously taking a little risk every day, enlarges your comfort zone and empowers you.

What do you have to lose? Go ahead, talk to that person who intimidates you; ask your boss for a raise if you deserve one; book dinner at a nice restaurant, even if it means eating alone; get out of the house and get involved! Every night before you go to sleep, plan the risk you're going to take the next day. And remember, the larger your comfort zone becomes, the less fear will factor into your thinking.

In other words – dare to dream!

Paul writes: "What advantage then hath the Jew? ...Much every way...unto them were committed the oracles of God" (Ro 3:1-2). God has spoken certain things concerning you. Those things are His *will* and His *purpose* for your life. Your job is to recognize them, believe them, carry them within you, and speak them often, because they give you a tremendous advantage.

Then Paul adds: "For what if some did not

believe? Shall their unbelief make the faith of God without effect? God forbid" (Ro 3:3-4). Get over the idea that the majority has to agree with you, or believe what God said about you. This is a difficult concept, especially in a democracy where others vote and the majority rules. The kingdom of God is a theocracy where only one vote counts – God's!

Refuse to put your dream on hold, waiting for everybody to get on the same page with you. Not only do they not have to support you, they don't even have to believe what God has told you.

You can't wait until others become comfortable with your dream before you pursue it. They can misunderstand you, talk about you, laugh at you, try to sabotage you, and you can *still* get there without them! Why? Because what God has spoken over your life, He will surely bring to pass: "Depend on it: God keeps his word" (Ro 3:4 TM).

What's the source of your dream?

You'd be surprised at the number of people who are tormented by a dream God never gave them – who waste their lives trying to do things He neither called nor equipped them to do.

What's the source of your dream? Did the most influential people in your life impose *their* dreams on you? "So-in-so always thought you'd make a wonderful doctor or lawyer." Stop and ask yourself, "Is it me? Others? The enemy? God?" It's not too late. If your dream's not of God, go back and seek Him and He'll give you one that is.

Look deep within yourself; who are you trying to impress? Are you trying to prove to your ex-husband or wife that you can make it without them? Or show your parents you're just as talented as your brother or sister? Or demonstrate to the world that you can overcome your beginnings and pull yourself up by your own bootstraps?

Your dream cannot be born out of your unresolved issues. That only breeds a need for control and recognition, and dooms you to fail.

Furthermore, if your dream is from God, you mustn't be impatient like Abraham and try to "make it happen." God's promises can never be fulfilled through fleshly effort. If only Abraham had waited he could've had Isaac, who represents "The blessing of the Lord which maketh rich – and adds no sorrow" (See Pr 10:22). No matter how long it takes, wait for God's timing, prepare yourself thoroughly, and go only when He says, "Go!"

What's the resource for your dream?

If God's the source of your dream, He'll also become the resource for it. Don't try to "get in" with certain people thinking they'll open the right door for you, then become resentful when it doesn't happen and develop a "you owe me" complex. Listen: "These are the words of him who…holds the key…What he opens no one can shut" (Rev 3:7 NIV).

God holds the key to your future, not others!

Once you understand that – God will challenge you to look *within* yourself. Why? *Because you always have enough to create what you need!* You may not recognize it yet, but it's there just waiting to be tapped. Stop saying, "I don't have what it takes." God's given you *everything* you need to get you where you ought to be!

Start looking in the mirror! Go ahead, hug yourself and announce, "I'm full of untapped potential." Until you pull out what God's placed within you, you'll live like a spectator envying the success of others.

It's not who *has* the most who wins – but who knows how to *use* it!

With all due respect to some of the world's greatest singers, there are folk washing dishes that could sing them under the table. The "biggies" only *got* big, by identifying what they had and making the most of it! So get rid of your false piety. Stop talking about what you *don't* have and begin using what you *do*. Listen: "It is God which worketh in you" (Ph 2:13). Today pull out your "God element" and put it to work! And when you do, keep these two things clearly in mind:

(1) *You don't have to have a dream that others consider great, for it to be important in God's eyes.* If your dream's to be a great parent that doesn't mean you don't have great faith, it just means you understand God's will for your life. All Moses' mother did was to give birth, but oh what a baby! God protected her son when she couldn't do a thing to help him. Then He brought her to Pharaoh's house and *paid* her to raise him. And when you discover your purpose, God will provide for you too! If you want to see

the money come, get the mission straight!

(2) *No matter how big your dream is, don't let it intimidate you!* As a child, Joseph dreamed of becoming a great leader – which first landed him in a pit, then a prison. "Where's your dream now, Joseph?" Understand this: your dream won't always look like it's coming together. Sometimes it'll seem to die before it springs to life. The Bible says that Abraham ignored the fact that his body was almost dead, believed God and fathered Isaac, even though biologically speaking it seemed like a lost cause.

Paul dreamed of winning the world for Christ and folks around him called him a fool. Did that derail him? Not one bit. "We are fools for Christ" he wrote (1 Co 4:10 NIV). God uses *radical* people! People who don't care what they look like, people who've survived difficult pasts, defied the odds, held on to their dream and declared, "My God is able!"

And you can be one of those people!

"I am too busy.
I have no time for worry."

SIR WINSTON CHURCHILL

9
Do It Now!

After his home had been burned to the ground and his family taken prisoner by the Amalekites, David could have thrown in the towel. But no, he stayed in the ring. When he asked God what his next move should be, God told him: "Go after them; you will recover everything that was taken" (1 Sa 30:8 TLB). When David followed God's instructions he ended up getting back his family, reestablishing his leadership and going on to become Israel's most beloved King!

Taking action is powerful!

God made it so that just a single step forward, robs fear of its power. In fact, one reason fear paralyzes so many of us is because we're waiting for some *outside* force to come and rescue us – when all the time God's calling *us* to act!

When you're afraid, the worst thing you can do is nothing. Fear can be a tremendous motivator, especially when it drives you to make changes leading to new levels of confidence and understanding.

Describing what he calls the "Cycle of Lethargy," psychologist David Burns says, "When I'm faced with a challenge and do nothing, it leads to distorted thoughts that I'm helpless, hopeless and beyond change. Those thoughts in turn lead to destructive emotions – loss of energy and motivation, damaged self-esteem and feeling overwhelmed. The end result is self-defeating behavior – procrastination, avoidance and escapism. These self-defeating behaviors feed on themselves and the whole cycle spirals downwards."

When you act and win it's wonderful! When you act and lose it's painful – but it's not failure. Failure is refusing to act at all!

Are you punching a time clock at a job you despise, or have no real passion for? Are you afraid to tackle a new venture in case you look foolish or can't make a living? Are you afraid to love again? To try again? Fear of failure can stop you from fulfilling your destiny by making you unavailable to God.

However, just as many people fear *success*, because then the pressure increases as others start expecting *more*. Before these people make any move they want an ironclad guarantee that everything will go according to plan. So they stay where they are – and stagnate! These are the ones who never go anywhere without a hot-water bottle, a thermometer, a parachute, and a raincoat!

Growth involves risk. Risk involves fear. And fear distorts our view of God. It tells you you're *not* in safe hands; that He's *not* big enough to take care of you. The question is, how will you ever *know*, unless you push beyond the fear and experience what God has for you?

At the end of the day all our "what ifs," become "what-might-have-beens." When you give in to fear you end up sitting in a comfortable chair in front of the TV, wondering, "What *could* I have accomplished, if only I hadn't been afraid?"

When you haven't accomplished what you'd hoped for, regret becomes a major pastime. The electrician wishes he'd been an accountant; the accountant wishes he'd been a doctor. Maybe you planned to leave a legacy, but to date all you've left is a trail of unfulfilled aspirations. Well it's not too late. You just have to be prepared to pursue your dream, hunt it down and sell out to get it. Don't listen to the fear-mongers and naysayers who settled for less and want you to do the same thing. Your goal isn't to live longer; it's to live *now!* Don't let fear rob you of your destiny. That's way too much to pay!

Charles Lindberg, the first man ever to fly the Atlantic said: "If I could fly for ten years before I was killed in a crash, it *still* would be a worthwhile trade for an ordinary lifetime. Who values life more; aviators who spend it doing what they love, or misers who dole it out like pennies throughout their antlike days?"

Who knows, your whole life may have been preparation for this very time! Look at Winston Churchill; instead of retiring after WWII, he went on to win a Nobel Prize in literature. When Heinrich Schliemann retired from business to look for Homer's legendary city of Troy – he found it!

Some of the saddest words in Scripture are, "The harvest is past, the summer is ended, and we are not saved" (Jer 8:20 NKJV).

Time passes …days slip by…years fly. Don't let fear stop you. Do it now while there's time!

10
FORTY FEAR-FIGHTERS

1 "Be anxious for nothing, but in everything by prayer…with thanksgiving let your requests be made known to God. And…peace…shall guard your hearts and…minds" (Ph 4:6-7 NASB).

2 "Casting…anxieties…worries…concerns, once and for all on Him, for he cares about you" (1 Pe 5:7 AMP).

3 "Be strong and courageous. Be not afraid or dismayed…for there is…with us…our God to help us" (2 Ch 32: 7-8 AMP).

4 "You are my help…I stay close to you; your right hand upholds me" (Ps 63:7-8 NCV).

5 "Because you have made the Lord your refuge…there shall no evil befall you, nor any…calamity come near" (Ps 91:9-10 AMP).

6 "He will call upon me, and I will answer…
I will be with him in trouble, I will
deliver…and honor him" (Ps 91:15 NIV).

7 "I will rescue you…declares the Lord; you
will not be handed over to those you fear"
(Jer 39:17 NIV).

8 "Fear not….When you pass through the
waters…they shall not overflow you. When
you walk through the fire, you shall not be
burned" (Is 43: 1-2 NKJV).

9 "The Lord is my…salvation…why should
I be afraid? The Lord protects me from
danger…why should I tremble"
(Ps 27:1 NLT).

10 "Be not afraid or dismayed…for the
battle is not yours, but God's"
(2 Ch 20:15 AMP).

11 "The Lord God is my Strength, my
personal bravery, and my invincible army.
He…will make me to walk [not…stand
still in terror…]" (Hab 3:19 AMP).

12 "In the world you have…distress and frustration; but …[take courage; be confident, certain, undaunted]…I have …[deprived it of power to harm you and have conquered it for you.]"
(Jn 16:33 AMP).

13 "I'll never let you down, never walk off and leave you" (Heb 13:5 TM).

14 "The Lord is my helper; I will not be afraid. What can man to do me?"
(He 13:6 NIV).

15 "I am the Lord…is there anything too hard for Me?" (Jer 32:27 AMP).

16 "Peace I now give…to you…[Stop allowing yourselves to be agitated… disturbed …fearful…intimidated… cowardly…unsettled]" (Jn 14: 27 AMP).

17 "I will lie down in peace and sleep, for though I am alone…Lord, you will keep me safe" (Ps 4:8 TLB).

18 "We trust you, Lord.... Others will tumble and fall, but we will be strong and stand firm" (Ps 20:7-8 CEV).

19 "Lean on, trust...and be confident in the Lord with all your heart...and do not rely on your own insight" (Pr 3:5 AMP).

20 "You are my hiding place; you will protect me...and surround me with songs of deliverance" (Ps 32:7 NIV).

21 "Have no fear of sudden disaster... for the Lord will be your confidence and will keep your foot from being snared" (Pr 3:25-26 NIV).

22 "The righteous cry out, and the Lord hears them; he delivers them from all their troubles" (Ps 34:17 NIV).

23 "Don't be afraid! I am the living one who died...And I hold the keys of death and the grave" (Rev 1:17-18 NLT).

24 "He is the faithful God, keeping his
covenant...to a thousand generations
of whose who love him and keep his
commands" (De 7: 9 NIV).

25 "You will be secure, because there is
hope; you will look about you and...rest
in safety" (Job 11:18 NIV).

26 "Nothing is impossible with God"
(Lk 1:37 NIV).

27 "God ...is my rock...my salvation...
my fortress, I will not be shaken"
(Ps 62:6 NIV).

28 "Blessed is the man...whose hope is the
Lord...For he shall be like a tree planted
by the waters...not...anxious in the year
of drought" (Jer 17: 7-8 AMP).

29 "They will fight against you, but...not
prevail...for I am with you to save...and
deliver you...from the grip of the terrible"
(Jer 15:20-21 NKJV).

30 "I have set the Lord...before me.
Because he is at my right hand, I will not
be shaken" (Ps 16:8 NIV).

31 "Even when I walk through the dark
valley of death, I will not be afraid, for you
are close beside me" (Ps 23:4 NLT).

32 "Our fears for today...worries about
tomorrow...even the powers of hell...
nothing in all creation will...separate us
from the love of God" (Ro 8:38-39 NLT).

33 "The plans I have for you...are...
for good and not for disaster, to give you
a future and a hope" (Jer 29:11 NLT).

34 "There is no fear in love...perfect love
casts out fear" (1 Jn 4:18 NKJV).

35 "Those who know your name will trust
in you, for you...have never forsaken those
who seek you" (Ps 9:10 NIV).

36 "I lay down and slept...for the Lord
sustained me. I will not be afraid of ten
thousand...who...set themselves against
me" (Ps 3:5-6 NKJV).

37 "The Lord himself watches over you…
stands beside you…keeps you from all
evil…preserves your life…keeps watch…
as you come and go" (Ps 121:5-8 NLT).

38 "I will…protect you wherever you go…
I will be with you constantly until I have
finished giving you everything I promised"
(Ge 28:15 NLT).

39 "He sends forth His Word…heals…
and (delivered) them from…destruction"
(Ps 107:20).

40 "If you will diligently hearken to the
voice of the Lord…and…do what is right
in His sight…I will put none of the diseases
upon you…for I am the Lord Who heals
you" (Ex 15:26 NKJV).

ACKNOWLEDGEMENTS

Feel The Fear And Do It Anyway, Susan Jeffers, Ph.D., Ballantine Books, New York: 1987

Age Erasers for Woman, Editors of Prevention Magazine Health Books: Rodale Press, Emmaus, Penn., 1994

You're Born an Original Don't Die a Copy, John L. Mason, Insight International, Tulsa, Ok., 1993

His Lady: Sacred Promises for God's Woman, T. D. Jakes, Berkeley Books, New York, 1999

More Language of Letting Go, Melody Beattie, Hazelden, Center City, Minn., 2000

Society of Human Resource Management and the Council of Public Relations Firms survey of 671 randomly selected human resource professional, USA Today, 10-08-02

He Still Moves Stones, Max Lucado, Word Publishing

Intercessory Prayer, Dutch Sheets, Regal Books, Ventura, Ca., 1996

Straight Talk on Fear, Joyce Meyer, Warner Faith, An AOL Time Warner Company. Printed in the United States of America, 1998

Be Healed in Jesus' Name, Joyce Meyer, Warner Faith, An AOL Time Warner Company, Printed in the United States of America, 2000

You Can't Afford the Luxury of a Negative Thought, Peter McWilliams, Prelude Press, Los Angeles, Ca., 1988

The Life God Rewards, Bruce Wilkinson, Multnomah

A Voice In The Wilderness, Joseph Bayly, Colorado Springs

How To Stop Worrying and Start Living, Dale Carnegie, Pocket Books, 1944